The Unexplained

CREATURES WALKING

Bigfoot, Yeti, and Apelike Cryptids

by Nathan Sommer and Stuart Webb

Minneapolis, Minnesota

Credits
Cover and title page, © anubhabroy/Adobe Stock and © Vegorus/Adobe Stock; 4BR, © Ash/Adobe Stock; 4–5, © Guido_Parmiggiani/Adobe Stock; 6MR, © andryuha1981/Shutterstock; 7TR, © Public Domain/Wikimedia; 7B, © FattalPhotography/Adobe Stock; 8–9, © Glasshouse Images/Getty Images; 10–11, © andreiuc88/Adobe Stock and © Mathias Weil/Adobe Stock and © AK082/Adobe Stock; 12MR, © Fortean/TopFoto; 13B, © Bearport Publishing; 15, © Google Maps; 15BR, © lesniewski/Adobe Stock; 16–17, © ondrejprosicky/Adobe Stock and © Sarawut/Adobe Stock and 17BR, © Fortean/Murphy/TopFoto; 18B, © Public Domain/Wikimedia; 19TR, © Associated Press; 20–21, © winterbilder/Adobe Stock; 21TR, © Fortean/TopFoto; 23, © stone36/Adobe Stock; 24–25, © olyasolodenko/Adobe Stock and © Thiago Santos/Adobe Stock; 26–27, © Yury Taranik/Adobe Stock; 27TR, © Public Domain/Wikimedia; 27BR, © Public Domain/Wikimedia; 28BL, © Public Domain/Wikimedia; 28–29, © Wayne/Adobe Stock and © evannovostro/Adobe Stock; 29T, © Express Newspapers/Getty Images; 29TR, © Public Domain/Wikimedia; 29MR, © Public Domain/Wikimedia; 30BL, © Daily Mail/Shutterstock; 30–31, © Daily Mail/Shutterstock; 31TR, © nomesart/Adobe Stock; 32MR, © Public Domain/Wikimedia; 32BR, © Public Domain/Wikimedia; 33BL, © Public Domain/Wikimedia; 34T, © Fernando Martinho/Adobe Stock; 35BR, © Bill Abbott/Wikimedia; 36B, © Orvar Belenus/Shutterstock; 37T, © PA Images/ Alamy; 39, © VarnakovR/Adobe Stock; 40–41, © Birdsincanberra.com/Adobe Stock; 43, © Andrey/Adobe Stock; 48, © Bearport Publishing

Photo Illustrations by Kim Jones.

Bearport Publishing Company Product Development Team
Publisher: Jen Jenson; Director of Product Development: Spencer Brinker; Managing Editor: Allison Juda; Associate Editor: Naomi Reich; Associate Editor: Tiana Tran; Art Director: Colin O'Dea; Designer: Kim Jones; Designer: Kayla Eggert; Product Development Specialist: Owen Hamlin

Statement on Usage of Generative Artificial Intelligence
Bearport Publishing remains committed to publishing high-quality nonfiction books. Therefore, we restrict the use of generative AI to ensure accuracy of all text and visual components pertaining to a book's subject. See BearportPublishing.com for details.

Library of Congress Cataloging-in-Publication Data is available at www.loc.gov or upon request from the publisher.

ISBN: 979-8-89232-886-9 (hardcover)
ISBN: 979-8-89232-916-3 (ebook)

For more information, write to Bearport Publishing, 5357 Penn Avenue South, Minneapolis, MN 55419.

Contents

A Mystery on Two Feet

People around the world have reported sightings of mysterious, apelike beings as far back as history can record. In the United States, these creatures are given names such as Bigfoot and Sasquatch. In Asia, they are called the Yeti or the Abominable Snowman. But just what are these humanlike beasts? And are they real or just a figment of our imagination?

A cryptid is a creature about which there are stories or legends but that has not been proven to exist based on science. Cryptozoologists are people who gather evidence on mysterious creatures in hopes of proving they are real. The Komodo dragon, platypus, and giant squid were all once considered cryptids. However, we now know these creatures are all very real.

Early Encounters

North American tales of Bigfoot and other humanlike cryptids date back hundreds of years to the native peoples and early European settlers. While each group had a different name for the beasts, they all described massive, furry, humanlike creatures that inhabited remote forested areas. Let's look back to the earliest encounters with these mysterious and sometimes terrifying beings. . . .

The Wendigo

Stories of a part-animal, part-human creature called the wendigo have long existed in the oral histories of North America's Algonquian-speaking groups. The creature is described as having horns or antlers, glowing eyes, and long claws. Legend has it that the wendigo uses its excellent hearing and sense of smell to stalk human victims in the cold, snowy woodlands of Canada and the northern United States. It is reported to grow larger the more it eats, reaching heights of up to 15 feet (4.6 m).

Wendigos are said to have a strong, awful odor that alerts people to their presence. According to stories, the creatures prey on people who are greedy, weak, or suffering from hunger. Some say the beings can be defeated only by using bullets or daggers made from silver, steel, or iron. Others insist a wendigo's heart must be removed and burned for the creature to be completely defeated.

Some stories say that the evil spirit of the wendigo is able to take control of human beings. It is said to possess people by biting them or entering their bodies through their dreams. The possessed are then said to become violent or even attempt to eat other people!

Unsettled Settlers

As early as 1793, European settlers in North America reported sightings of what was called a hairy ape-man. In 1811, British-Canadian fur trader David Thompson came face-to-face with what he described as a group of humanlike, hairy giants while camping in what is today Washington State. Thompson wrote in his diary that the creatures were more than 7 ft. (2.1 m) tall with long, black hair. He said they spoke to one another using whistling sounds and seemed unafraid of Thompson's presence after spotting him. In 1847, miners in California's Sierra Nevada Mountains claimed to have seen a group of similar creatures, but they said those gorilla-like wild men attacked them.

David Thompson explored more than 100,000 miles (161,000 km) through North America between 1785 and 1812.

The Battle of Ape Canyon

One of the most famous Bigfoot encounters occurred in July 1924, just southeast of Washington's Mount St. Helens. Fred Beck, Marion Smith, and three other men had been staying at a cabin and mining gold in the area for more than two years. According to the men, they began hearing loud banging and strange whistling sounds at night coming from the woods around the cabin. They claimed to have found huge footprints at nearby water sources, the largest measuring 19 inches (48 cm) long. The prints were too large to belong to any animal they knew of.

Ape Canyon is a gorge that narrows to almost 8 ft. (2.4 m) at its smallest point. Its nearby trail is popular with hikers and mountain bikers.

The encounter these gold prospectors had with Bigfoot became so famous that the area where it occurred became known as Ape Canyon. Since then, many others in Washington have claimed to have spotted the creature. Washington State leads the world in Bigfoot sightings with more than 2,000—and counting!

These occurrences alarmed the men enough that they began carrying their rifles with them into the woods. One day, Beck and Smith were collecting water from a spring near their cabin when their fears suddenly became reality. The men said they spotted a hairy creature watching them from behind a pine tree about 300 ft. (90 m) away. According to Beck, the creature had long blackish-brown hair covering its body. It appeared to stand more than 7 ft. (2.1 m) tall, and they estimated it weighed more than 400 pounds (180 kg).

Startled, Beck fired three rifle shots in the direction of the creature but hit only the pine tree in front of it. As Beck fired more shots, the creature quickly ran away down a nearby canyon before disappearing from view. Beck and Smith ran back to their cabin to tell the others what had happened. It was nearly nightfall. Although they were afraid and wanted to leave, the men did not want to risk meeting the creatures in the dark. They decided to stay one more night and planned to leave the area the next morning.

After discussing their strange encounter, the men tried to settle down and go to bed, looking forward to leaving the next day. Unfortunately, their struggles with the beasts had just begun. Around midnight, the men were awoken by booming thuds against the outside of their cabin—blows strong enough to break pieces off the wall. When they looked outside, the men said they saw three of the huge creatures. The apelike beasts were hurling rocks and throwing their giant, powerful bodies against the cabin, trying to get inside!

The front door on the cabin shook as the creatures repeatedly slammed against it. The men tried to use a long pole to barricade the door, but it didn't help. One of the apelike creatures reached through the broken wall to grab hold of an axe inside the cabin. Two others were able to climb onto the cabin's roof.

The attack continued throughout the night. Finally, daylight arrived, and the creatures retreated back into the woods. Eventually, the terrified men left the cabin to begin their escape. As they set off down a nearby trail, the men saw one of the creatures emerge from the trees about 240 ft. (70 m) away. Beck had his rifle and fired, and this time he did not miss.

According to Beck, he shot the creature three times. It collapsed and tumbled over the cliff of the nearby canyon, falling more than 400 ft. (120 m). The men completed their escape to nearby Spirit Lake without seeing any other creatures along the way. News quickly spread throughout the area about the mountain devils—creatures that the unlucky prospectors had faced off against.

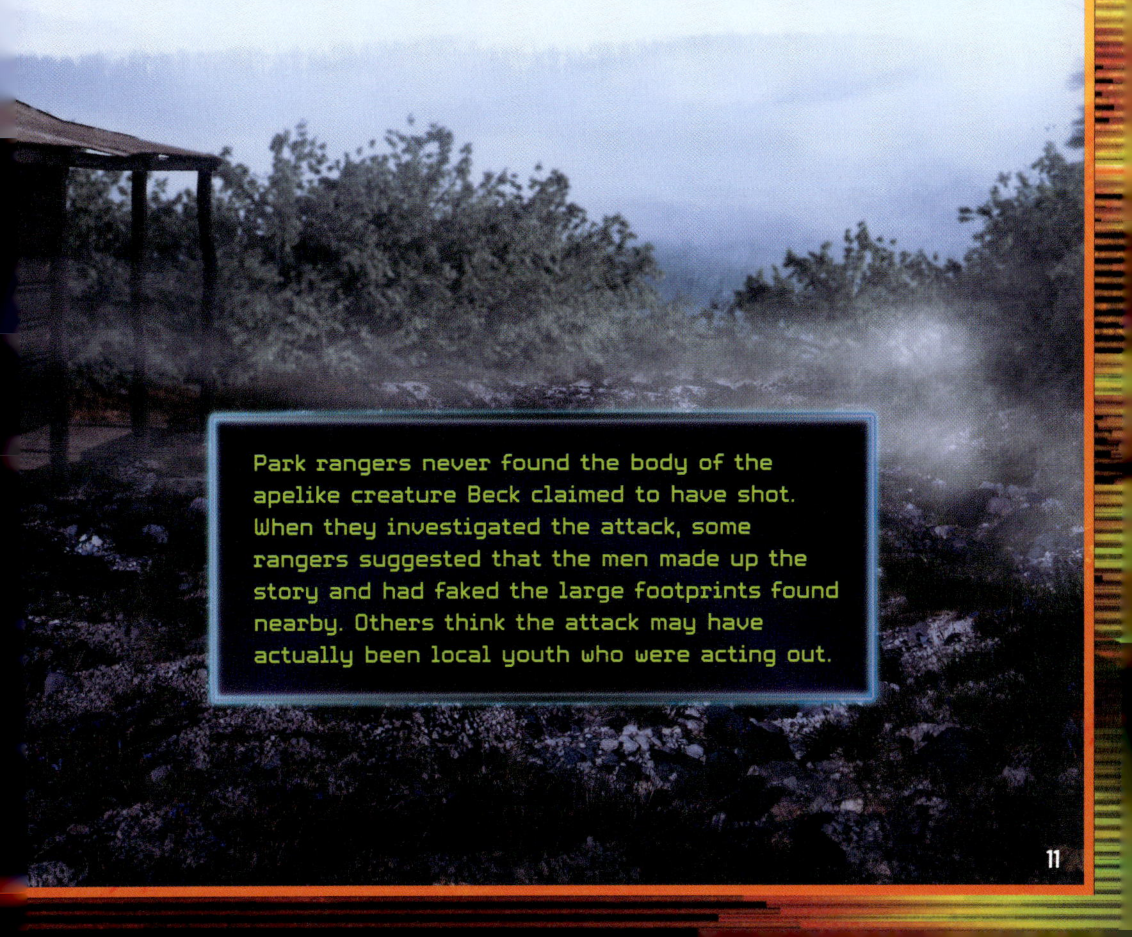

Park rangers never found the body of the apelike creature Beck claimed to have shot. When they investigated the attack, some rangers suggested that the men made up the story and had faked the large footprints found nearby. Others think the attack may have actually been local youth who were acting out.

Kidnapped by Bigfoot

In 1957, a lumberjack named Albert Ostman shared an extraordinary story that he claimed had taken place more than 30 years earlier. Ostman said that during the summer of 1924, he was camping near British Columbia's Toba Inlet. Every morning, he noticed that his campsite had been disturbed during the night. Assuming it was animals searching for food, Ostman decided to sleep with his rifle inside his sleeping bag.

That night, Ostman woke up to the sensation of being lifted while still in his sleeping bag! He claimed that a large, upright creature carried and dragged him for hours before eventually dropping him. When he peeked out, Ostman was shocked to see four tall, muscular, apelike beings staring back at him. Ostman believed he had been taken to a remote mountain valley, which he assumed was the creatures' home. According to him, the creatures had humanlike faces with sloped foreheads and no visible necks. The group appeared to be a family—a father, mother, son, and daughter. The creatures slept under blankets made of woven bark and moss.

Ostman is not the only person who claims to have been kidnapped by Bigfoot. Canadian fur trapper Muchlat Harry said he was captured by a group of about 20 similar creatures in 1928. Harry reported seeing piles of gnawed bones around their camp. He claims to have been able to escape before finding out what—or who—the bones belonged to.

Ostman claimed he lived with this family of creatures for nearly a week. They observed him closely as he ate from his knapsack and explored their home. Though they didn't harm him, they also didn't allow him to leave. Whenever Ostman tried to exit the valley through the only visible opening, the father creature blocked the path. As his food supply dwindled, Ostman realized he needed a plan to escape. He had only six bullets left, and he doubted they would be enough against these massive beings.

Ostman claimed that the creatures enjoyed the taste of his food. He decided to trick the father by offering him a container filled with tobacco instead of food. The father creature ate the tobacco and became violently ill. Taking advantage of the situation, Ostman managed to escape while the sick creature was too weak and distracted to stop him. Ostman kept his story a secret for more than 30 years, saying he feared that no one would believe him. However, as more people began reporting Bigfoot sightings, Ostman decided to finally share his extraordinary experience.

Footprints at Bluff Creek

While tales of hairy, apelike beings have been reported for centuries, the name *Bigfoot* was first coined in 1958 after a series of mysterious events at Bluff Creek in Six Rivers National Forest in northern California. Construction manager Ray Wallace and his crew of 30 men had been tasked with building a road to support the area's logging industry. Over time, the team claimed to experience increasingly bizarre incidents. At first, tools would go missing overnight. Later, they discovered that heavy equipment had been mysteriously dragged away from the worksite and left up a nearby hill.

Wallace and his crew didn't think much of these occurrences until the morning of August 27, 1958. As on other mornings, they arrived to find their worksite disturbed. However, this time, the intruder had left behind massive, humanlike footprints. Jerry Crew, a member of the team, was the first to notice the prints near his bulldozer. Initially, he assumed they belonged to a bear or perhaps a coworker. But as he examined them more closely, Crew realized the footprints were far larger than expected.

The footprints Crew discovered measured 7 in. (18 cm) wide and nearly 16 in. (41 cm) long. After following the tracks, Crew became convinced they belonged to a giant, humanlike creature. He shared his findings with his coworkers, who then began recalling other strange incidents from the area. Some remembered the mysterious disappearance of a gigantic 50-gallon (190-L) oil drum. Others spoke of a 700-lb. (320-kg) object that had been hurled down a ravine. The team began referring to the creature responsible as Bigfoot.

Wallace also claimed to have measured the movements of Bigfoot by following the creature's tracks. According to Wallace, Bigfoot's stride covered 50 in. (130 cm) per step while walking. While running, Wallace said the creature could cover nearly 10 ft. (3 m) per stride!

In early October 1958, more enormous footprints appeared around Wallace's worksite. This time, Wallace decided to create a plaster cast of the prints to show the *Humboldt Times*, the local newspaper. Photos of the cast, along with stories of the strange events at Bluff Creek, quickly spread across Canada and the United States, and the legend of Bigfoot was born.

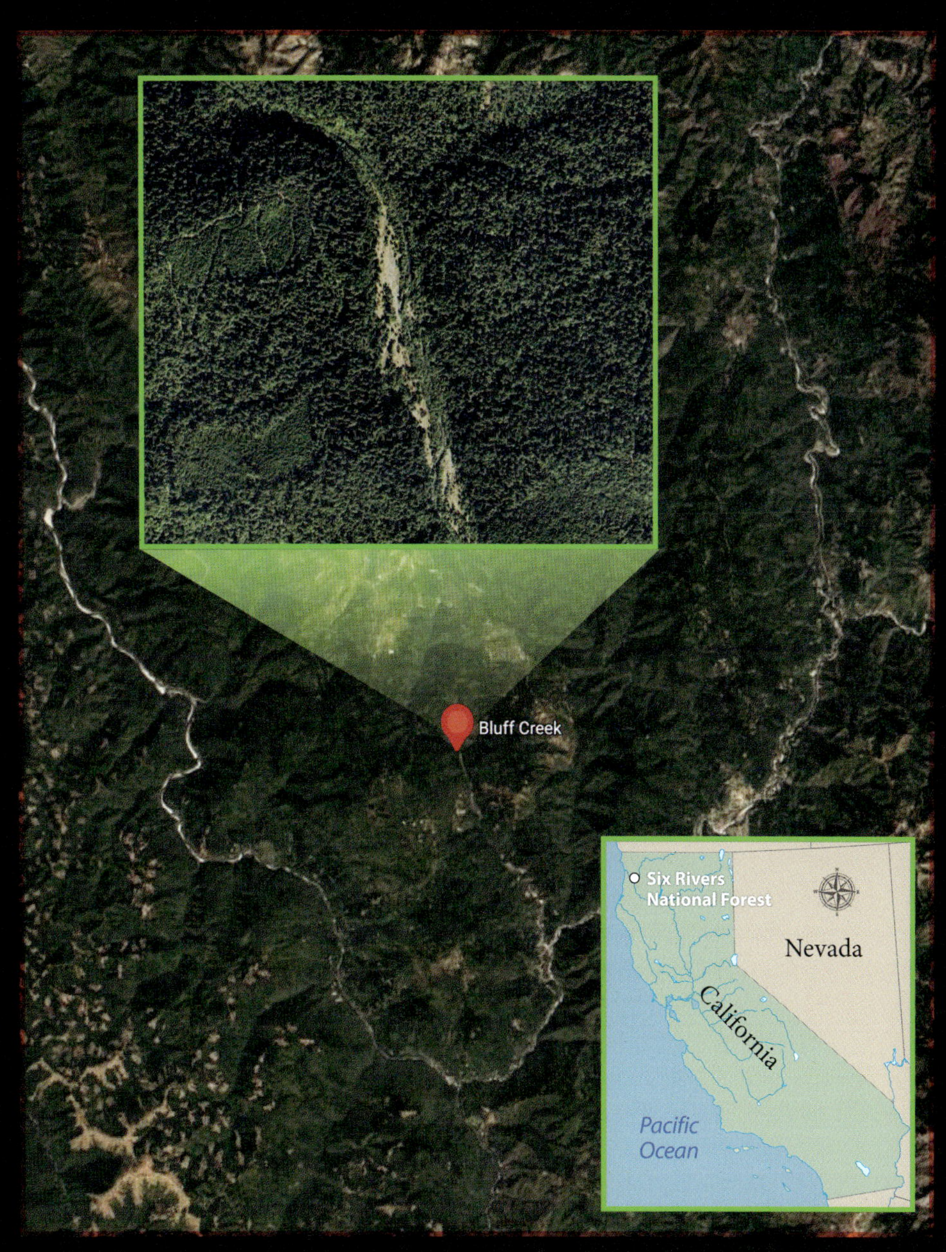

Bluff Creek is in Six Rivers National Forest in northern California.

As the strange events continued, Wallace and his crew increasingly felt as though they were being watched. Some workers began carrying guns for protection. The situation reached its peak on October 12, 1958, when workers Ray Kerr and Leslie Breazeale claimed they came face-to-face with the mysterious creature responsible for the footprints. According to Breazeale, he was dozing in the passenger seat during a late-night drive when Kerr suddenly slammed on the brakes. Breazeale awoke just in time to see a large, hairy figure—Bigfoot—illuminated in the headlights as it crossed the road about 40 ft. (12 m) in front of the startled men.

Kerr estimated that the creature stood over 8 ft. (2.4 m) tall. He described it as running upright like a human, with long, hairy arms swinging by its sides. After the creature vanished into the nearby woods, the men inspected the tracks it left behind and saw that they matched the footprints that had appeared around their construction site. To Kerr and Breazeale, this encounter confirmed their coworkers' suspicions—they had seen Bigfoot in the flesh.

As word spread, skeptics and investigators from around the world flocked to Bluff Creek, hoping to catch a glimpse of Bigfoot themselves. Bob Titmus, a friend of Jerry Crew, was among the first to actively search for the creature. He and other investigators spent countless hours collecting footprints, eyewitness accounts, and hair samples. More plaster casts were made, and scientists agreed that the footprints did not belong to a bear, as some had speculated.

The mystery of the footprints was partially resolved many years later, following Ray Wallace's death. His children revealed that their father had used a pair of oversized wooden feet to create the fake Bigfoot tracks. However, believers argue that Wallace was only responsible for some of the tracks, as footprints were reported even when he was out of town. They also point out that the faked footprints cannot explain the many other strange occurrences and Bigfoot sightings in the area.

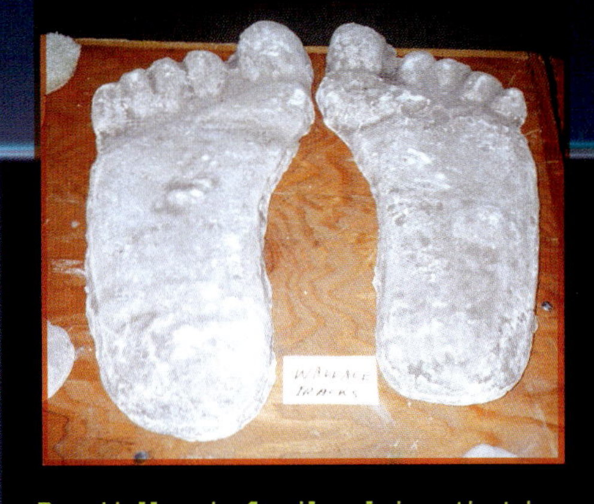

Ray Wallace's family claims that he was a prankster. His critics claim he created the footprints because his team had fallen behind in their work. They say Wallace needed a reason to extend the deadline of their project and that the alleged Bigfoot was an easy culprit for him to blame.

A Famous Film

In October 1967, filmmakers Roger Patterson and Bob Gimlin set out for Bluff Creek, driven by reports of new, gigantic footprints in the area. Patterson had heard about the footprints from a local Bigfoot investigator, and he was eager to capture them on film. However, by the time Patterson and Gimlin arrived, heavy rains had washed away the supposed Bigfoot tracks. Despite this setback, the two decided to stay and continue exploring the area. What they encountered soon surpassed any original expectations.

On October 20, 1967, Patterson and Gimlin ventured into a rugged, remote canyon near Bluff Creek. As they rounded a corner blocked by fallen trees, they claimed to have spotted a Bigfoot crouching near a creek about 80 ft. (25 m) away. The creature quickly noticed the men and stared directly back at them. Patterson immediately grabbed his camera and began filming. What happened next is considered by many to be the most significant piece of evidence supporting the existence of Bigfoot.

The film footage captured by Patterson and Gimlin of a creature looking at the camera is the most famous Bigfoot evidence ever presented.

Patterson managed to film the dark, hairy creature for nearly a minute as it walked along the creek's bank, gradually moving away from him and into the surrounding woods. In the most famous shot from the footage, the creature turns mid-stride to glance at the camera before continuing on its way. The men quickly rushed to the nearby town of Eureka to have their video footage developed. News of the film spread rapidly among Bigfoot researchers, and soon millions of people were viewing the video. For many, Bigfoot was no longer just a story.

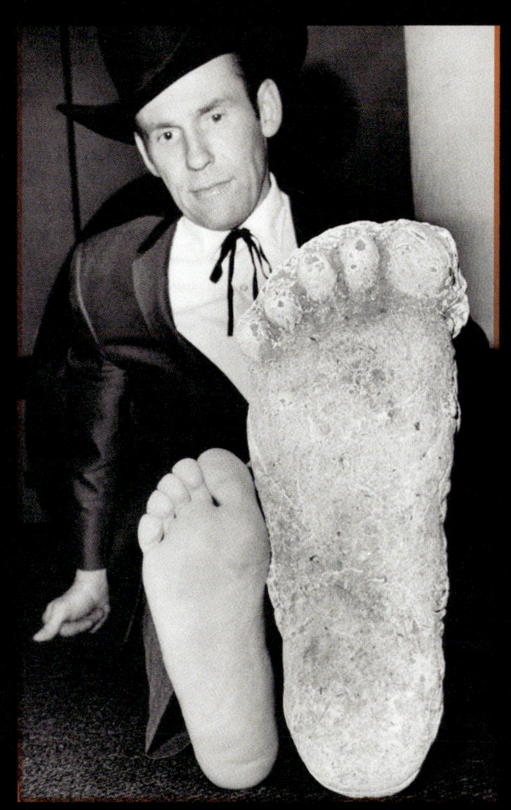

Roger Patterson compares his foot to a cast said to be from Bigfoot.

Though Patterson and Gimlin's footage has never been conclusively proven to be a hoax, it has sparked considerable controversy. In 2002, a costume designer named Phillip Morris claimed that he had sold Patterson an apelike costume shortly before the film was shot. A man named Bob Heironimus asserted that Patterson paid him to wear the costume. However, skeptics of the hoax theory argue that faking the film would have been nearly impossible using the special effects technology and costumes available in 1967. Further studies have struggled to replicate the creature's unique posture and gait using human actors. In addition, Roger Patterson passed a lie detector test regarding the incident before his death in 1972.

Bigfoot has allegedly been caught on camera several other times. In 1994, Paul Freeman recorded a hairy, humanlike figure crossing a wooded path in Walla Walla, Washington. Footage shot in 1995 shows what appears to be a Bigfoot in a car's headlights on a rainy night in northern California. No footage thus far has matched the quality of Patterson and Gimlin's.

The Skunk Ape

The southeastern United States is home to its own mysterious, hairy, humanlike creatures, known as skunk apes. For centuries, Florida's native Seminole population referred to these beings as *Esti Capcaki*, meaning tall man. Allegedly standing around 7 ft. (2.1 m) tall and weighing up to 500 lb. (230 kg), skunk apes are notorious for the extremely foul odor they emit—a pungent smell of skunk, rotting eggs, and feces. Witnesses claim that the stench often lingers long after the creatures have vanished from sight.

Those who have encountered skunk apes describe them as having wide, flat faces with large noses and deep-set eyes that glow bright green in the dark, much like a gorilla's. Unlike Bigfoot, skunk apes have been observed hunched over and moving quickly on all fours in a distinctly apelike manner. Witnesses also report that their bodies are covered in shaggy, reddish-brown fur.

A Florida couple claimed to have taken this photo of a skunk ape in 2000 when the creature supposedly showed up on their back porch.

The first recorded encounter with the skunk ape by European settlers occurred in 1818, when a newspaper article described man-sized monkeys raiding food stores and following fishermen along the shoreline near what is now Apalachicola, Florida. In 1900, a large, apelike creature was reportedly seen on an island in the Mississippi River near Hannibal, Missouri. Then, in 1942, a man in Tallahassee, Florida, claimed that one of these creatures clung to his car for miles before eventually leaping off and disappearing into the woods.

Sightings of skunk apes became more frequent in the 1960s, coinciding with construction projects that reportedly encroached on the creatures' natural habitat. It is believed that these disruptions forced the skunk apes deeper into Florida's Everglades. Since then, they have most often been spotted near roadsides by drivers traveling through rural areas with dense forests and wetlands. While skeptics suggest that witnesses might be mistaking bears or wild hogs for skunk apes, those who claim to have encountered the creatures insist they are unlike anything they have ever seen before.

Richard Lee Smith claimed to have hit a skunk ape with his car near Pembroke Pines, Florida, in January 1974. Smith said that after it was hit, the tall, hairy creature stood up, roared, and charged at his car. Smith sped away, but witnesses—including police officers—reported seeing a giant, limping creature along nearby roadways for hours afterward.

The Fouke Monster

On the night of May 1, 1971, Elizabeth Ford claimed to have an extraordinary experience. She said she was napping on the sofa in her new home in Fouke, Arkansas, when she was abruptly awakened by the sound of a window sliding open. To her shock, a large, hairy arm with clawed fingers reached through the window moments later. Elizabeth claimed to have peered outside and saw an apelike face with piercing red eyes staring back at her. Terrified, she screamed, which alerted her husband, Bobby, who was just returning from a hunting trip. Bobby grabbed his shotgun and fired several shots, causing the creature to flee.

However, the horror was far from over. The couple reported that later that night, the creature returned and forcefully kicked in the family's back door. Bobby said he fired at it once more and then went to investigate the back porch. There, the creature seized him by the shoulders and attacked. Bobby described the creature as breathing heavily as it dragged him down to the backyard. After a fierce struggle, Bobby managed to break free and run straight through his front door to hide inside the house.

The following morning, Bobby was taken to the hospital to treat deep claw marks on his body. When local police examined the Ford residence, they discovered large, unidentified tracks around the yard and claw marks on the porch. Disturbed by the night's events, Bobby and Elizabeth chose to move out of their new home after having lived there for only one week. Their unsettling encounter was reported in local newspapers, which dubbed the creature the Fouke Monster.

Reports of the Fouke Monster persist to this day. In 2023, Fouke resident Denny Roberts claimed to have seen a large, orangutan-like creature in the woods while driving. Earlier that year, a deer hunter reported seeing a similar creature watching him from behind a tree for approximately 15 minutes. Residents in the city's more isolated areas say they sometimes hear the monster's howls late at night.

Tales like that of the Fords are particularly unsettling, since Bigfoot-like creatures are usually said to be shy and avoid human interactions. The apelike beasts allegedly found in the southeastern United States are reported to be the most hostile toward humans. Some people think this may be true if the creatures are driven by hunger.

Momo the Monster

In July 1971, Joan Mills and Mary Ryan stopped for a picnic near Louisiana, Missouri. They said that just as they were about to enjoy their meal, they were overwhelmed by a terrible odor. Suddenly, an apelike creature emerged from the nearby bushes. The creature was covered in black hair and made a gurgling noise as it approached. Terrified, the women hurried into their car, but in their panic, they left the keys behind and couldn't drive away.

The creature approached their car and, to their horror, began to stroke it and try to open the locked doors. Fortunately, it was unable to get inside. The women soon managed to scare it off by honking the horn, but not before the creature raided their picnic and ate some of their food. It then retreated into the bushes and disappeared.

The same creature was sighted again in the area in July 1972. That summer, Doris Harrison reported that she heard a scream coming from outside her house. When she looked out the window, she saw a hairy, black creature standing next to her younger brothers in the nearby woods. Harrison said the creature was standing upright like a human and was covered in blood and holding a dead dog. It retreated into the woods, leaving behind clumps of hair and a foul odor strong enough to make their family dog sick.

The mysterious beast, later named Momo the Monster by locals, continued to cause alarm. Neighbors reported missing pets, strange footprints, and unsettling animalistic growls and screams coming from the nearby woods. Witnesses who saw Momo described it as having a large, pumpkin-shaped head with glowing orange eyes.

Some believe creatures such as Momo the Monster belong to a subspecies of Bigfoot that exist in the midwestern and eastern United States. Reports of this creature, called the Eastern Bigfoot, detail its aggressive behavior compared with reports of Bigfoots of the Northwest. Eastern Bigfoots are thought to be less shy since they live in closer proximity to humans.

Yeti: Monster on the Mountain

Stories of a gigantic, apelike beast living in the mountains have been told for hundreds of years. Native Siberians spoke of the *chuchuyna*, a furry, Neanderthal-like creature that raided barns at night and consumed human flesh. In the Himalayan mountains, ancient people spoke of a similar creature that roamed the snowy peaks, protecting them from evil. They called it the *metoh-kangmi*, which was later translated as the Abominable Snowman. Over time, this creature became widely known as the Yeti.

Those who have encountered the Yeti claim it stands up to 15 ft. (4.5 m) tall. It is described as having a muscular build, shaggy white fur, and long arms that reach its knees. The creature is said to have a broad forehead, glowing orange eyes, and razor-sharp teeth. Its large feet supposedly leave deep tracks in the snow.

European mountaineers first reported seeing the Yeti in 1832. British climber B. H. Hodgson said that guides traveling with him in northern Nepal were frightened by a tall, wild man covered in long hair. Hodgson thought the guides had mistaken an orangutan for the Yeti. In 1889, British explorer L. A. Waddell found enormous, humanlike footprints in northeast India. The Tibetans with him claimed the tracks belonged to a dangerous beast, which made Waddell decide to leave the area quickly.

Climber B. H. Hodgson

In the early 1900s, Mary MacDonald was hiking near the Tibetan border when her trek was interrupted by a monstrous roar echoing off the nearby rocks. When she turned to ask her local guides about the sound, she found they had abandoned their gear and were running away. MacDonald eventually caught up with them miles down the path. They told her the roar came from a *metoh-kangmi* that was warning them to stay away.

Explorer L. A. Waddell

The name *Yeti* comes from the Tibetan word *yet-teh*, which translates to bearlike in English. Tibetans use this word to describe many large animals found in the country's mountains. This sometimes leads to confusion when visitors hear stories about aggressive animals, often bears, in the area.

Explorer Charles Howard-Bury

During a Mount Everest expedition in 1921, British explorer Charles Howard-Bury became one of the first to claim he saw the Yeti with his own eyes. Howard-Bury's crew saw large, humanlike figures walking across a snowfield about 20,000 ft. (6,000 m) above sea level. When they reached the area, they found extremely large tracks resembling those of huge, barefoot humans.

In 1925, Greek photographer N. A. Tombazi reported another Yeti sighting in the Himalayas. Tombazi claimed that while exploring 15,000 ft. (4,600 m) above sea level, he saw a naked, dark, humanlike creature walking upright about 300 yards (270 m) away. Tombazi claimed the creature seemed to be searching for food, occasionally stopping to pluck leaves from bushes and chew on the branches.

Eric Shipton was a moutaineer who set out to discover new routes up Mount Everest. (*Clockwise from top right*: Eric Shipton; the famous photograph of a supposed Yeti footprint; Shipton's camp in the Himalayan Mountains)

The Yeti gained worldwide attention in 1951 when British mountaineer Eric Shipton acquired photographic evidence to support what many had previously reported. Shipton, who was in the Himalayas to map new routes up Mount Everest, found more than just new pathways. While exploring the Menlung Basin, he and his partner discovered a trail of strange footprints in the snow. The footprints measured 13 in. (33 cm) long and had oddly shaped toes. Shipton took a photo of the tracks next to an ice pick to give perspective as to their size.

Shipton's photos became famous and were published in newspapers worldwide. Many saw this as proof of the Yeti's existence. Critics, however, argued that the footprints were either faked or the result of animal tracks distorted by melting snow. Others suggested the tracks might belong to a local person with a physical disability. Despite the controversy, Shipton's findings sparked a global discussion, and the Yeti became a household name.

British journalist Henry Newman is credited with creating the nickname *the Abominable Snowman*. This was his translation of the ancient Himalayan name *metoh-kangmi*, which actually means man-bear snowman. While Newman's translation was not completely accurate, it became permanently linked to the mysterious creature.

An Expedition for Evidence

Eric Shipton's photos of the footprint sparked a surge of alleged Yeti sightings in the Himalayas. Public interest grew so high that in 1954, the British newspaper the *Daily Mail* launched an expedition to prove the creature's existence once and for all. They assembled a team of more than 350 people, including mountaineers, local guides, journalists, and zoologists. The mission, known as the Snowman Expedition, aimed to search the mountains, gather information about the Yeti, and—if possible—capture one.

Equipped with tranquilizer guns and a cage, the Snowman Expedition team spent 15 weeks exploring the mountains, covering vast distances. They tracked and photographed numerous large footprints but did not spot a single Yeti. The team also visited Buddhist monasteries that claimed to possess parts of the creature. In Pangboche, Nepal, explorers were shown what they were told was a Yeti hand, while in Khumjung, Nepal, another monastery displayed an alleged 300-year-old Yeti scalp.

A British explorer is shown an alleged Yeti scalp during the expedition in 1954.

Members of the Snowman Expedition in search of the Yeti

American explorer Peter Byrne made significant efforts to smuggle a crusted, black finger he claimed to be from a Yeti out of Nepal. However, in 2011, DNA testing revealed that the finger came from a large human hand. Analysis of the supposed Yeti scalp showed it was actually made from the skin and hair of a wild Himalayan goat. To this day, no definitive evidence of the Yeti's existence has been found.

Rumored Yeti sightings continue each year in the snowy peaks of Asia and Siberia. Some believe these creatures might be survivors of a small population of large apes that once lived in the Himalayas and were thought to be extinct. Fossil records of extinct Asian apes show that some stood up to 9.8 ft. (3 m) tall. Whether ape or something else, much about the elusive Yeti remains unknown.

The largest ape ever to walk Earth was *Giganopithecus blacki*. Could the Yeti be a distant relative of this extinct primate?

In February 1959, nine hikers on an expedition in Russia's Ural Mountains died under mysterious circumstances in what is now known as the Dyatlov Pass incident. Some believe that an angry Yeti might have caused their deaths. The hikers' tent was found cut open from the inside, as if they had been trying to escape something. Several of the hikers had suffered blunt force injuries to their heads and chests, and some were missing body parts when discovered.

The Maricoxi of South America

Witnesses claim that the rainforests of South America are home to various hairy, apelike creatures. Depending on the region, these creatures go by different names, but Maricoxi is the general term used. Reports suggest that these creatures are more aggressive than other cryptids and often react poorly to human encounters. Some are said to scream loudly and charge at intruders as a scare tactic, while others attack humans on sight.

First Sighting

One of the earliest written records of the Maricoxi comes from the 1769 accounts of American explorer Edward Bancroft. Locals in northeastern South America described humanlike beings covered in short black fur that stood upright at about 5 ft. (1.5 m) tall. Bancroft noted that these creatures were greatly feared by the native peoples in the area.

Edward Bancroft

Achi

German explorer Alexander von Humboldt received similar reports while mapping Venezuela's Orinoco River in 1825. The Tamarac people spoke of a dangerous hairy man in the woods called *Achi*, which was said to kidnap women and eat human flesh. The Maipure people referred to this being as the *Vasitiri*, meaning great devil. Von Humboldt reported that both locals and foreign missionaries feared the creature.

Alexander von Humboldt

Whistles in the Forest

In 1876, Canadian explorer Charles Barrington Brown described a strange, animalistic noise he heard while traveling along Guyana's Mazaruni River. Brown was startled by a loud, repeated whistling sound. His local guides explained that the noise was made by a powerful, hairy wild man living in the forest. To avoid the fearsome creature, Brown and his guides crossed to the other side of the river.

During his travels, Brown encountered another man who claimed to have had a close encounter with a male and female Maricoxi. According to the man, he accidentally stumbled upon the creatures while chopping timber. The man claimed the Maricoxi immediately attacked him, scratching him severely, but he managed to defend himself and ultimately escape.

The ape photographed by de Loys

Louis François de Loys was a Swiss geologist who claimed to have discovered a previously unknown primate during a 1920 survey expedition in Venezuela. His photograph of the creature became famous and sparked more interest in South American Maricoxi. Today, most scientists believe de Loys' photo was a hoax, showing only the body of a spider monkey.

A Village of Creatures

British geographer Percy Fawcett led an expedition into the rainforests of Brazil's Mato Grosso region in 1914. During their exploration, Fawcett's group allegedly stumbled upon a village inhabited by enormous apelike creatures. Fawcett described them as having human stature but being as hairy as dogs. Alarmed, the creatures of the village quickly armed themselves with bows and arrows. Fawcett frightened them off by firing his gun at their feet. The villagers retreated but shot arrows at Fawcett's team as they narrowly escaped.

Fawcett and his crew disappeared while searching for a lost city near Brazil's Amazon Rainforest in 1925. Their bodies were never found. Some think they may have fallen victim to the hairy, humanlike creatures they first met in 1914 or to one of the other man-eating Maricoxi rumored to be in the area.

Maricoxi Attacks

In 1920, François de Loys and his team camped near Colombia's Tarra River. During their rest, de Loys reported an attack by two apelike animals about 5 ft. (1.5 m) tall. The creatures screeched, waved branches threateningly, and threw their feces at de Loys' group. In self-defense, his team shot and killed one of the attackers. Upon examining the body, they found it was humanlike, without a tail, and larger than other primates in the region.

In 1968, Croatian explorer Pino Turolla heard stories about Maricoxi attacking a father and son in eastern Venezuela. Locals said the father escaped but the child was clubbed to death. Three years later, Turolla claimed to have seen two Maricoxi fleeing from him in the same area.

Continued Sightings

Maricoxi sightings continue throughout South America today. Recently, reports have emerged of a large, slothlike creature called the *Mapinguari*, which is said to be incredibly smelly and bulletproof. Witnesses describe the *Mapinguari* as larger than any known mammal in South America. Brazilian berry pickers who saw the creature in 2014 reported it was more than 6 ft. (1.8 m) tall with a single glowing red eye.

Skeptics argue that most Maricoxi sightings are cases of mistaken identity. They suggest sightings of the creatures could be people witnessing undiscovered human tribes living in the rainforest or simply large primates. Some believe the *Mapinguari* could be a species of large ground sloths previously thought to be extinct.

Huge ground sloths once roamed throughout North and South America.

Island Creatures

On the Indonesian island of Sumatra, there are reports of small, hairy creatures known as *Orang Pendek*, which means short person. These beings are described as having humanlike faces, muscular shoulders, and reddish or dark gray hair. Witnesses say the *Orang Pendek* stands 3 to 5 ft. (0.9 to 1.5 m) tall and lives on the forest floor. Often called little Bigfoots, they are not aggressive toward humans but are said to be very strong for their size.

One of the earliest written accounts of the *Orang Pendek* came from Dr. Edward Jacobson in 1916. Local hunters told Jacobson they had seen one of these creatures from about 60 ft. (18 m) away. When the creature noticed the hunters, it ran away on two legs, similar to a human. Jacobson thought this was unusual because the island's apes would usually climb trees to escape. When he investigated, he reportedly found tiny, humanlike footprints on the forest floor.

This cast of a footprint and accompanying drawings are thought to be evidence of the existence of an *Orang Pendek*.

In 1923, a Dutch explorer named van Herwaarden claimed to have spotted an *Orang Pendek* while hunting wild pigs. He described seeing a dark, hairy creature standing on a tree branch, trying to stay hidden. As van Herwaarden and the *Orang Pendek* stared at each other cautiously, he noted its humanlike eyes and ears. The creature's face did not resemble an ape's at all. Eventually, the *Orang Pendek* became nervous, ran away, and made a noise that sounded like *hoo-hoo*!

In 1990, English researcher Debbie Martyr reported seeing an *Orang Pendek* as well. She described it as having a muscular build like a human athlete with powerful upper body strength. Although Martyr has spent years trying to prove the existence of an *Orang Pendek*, she has not yet captured photographic evidence. Local farmers in Sumatra still claim that these little Bigfoots often raid their crops.

Orang Pendeks are allegedly not the only mysterious creatures living on Sumatra. The island is also rumored to be home to another group of small beings called the *Orang Kardil*, meaning tiny men. They are said to be hairless, humanlike creatures that hunt using poisoned bamboo spears and are known to steal food from people around Sumatra.

Wild Creatures of Asia

Central and Southeast Asia have long been rumored to be home to large creatures that are neither fully human nor animal. These beings are said to have thick reddish-brown fur covering their bodies, except for their faces, feet, and chests. Witnesses describe them as being more like cavemen than Bigfoot, with pointed skulls, slanted foreheads, and powerful jaws. Over time, these creatures have been known by many names, but they are most commonly referred to as the *Yeren* in China and the *Almas* in Mongolia and Russia.

In the 1430s, German explorer Johann Schiltberger wrote about wild people living in Asia's remote mountains. He described them as running around like animals, eating grass and scavenging for other food. In 1664, a journal published a list of wild animals found in China and Mongolia, including a drawing of a furry, humanlike figure standing upright. The description of this figure suggested it had the body of a man and was known for enormous strength.

In the 1800s, a man in Abkhazia claimed to have captured and domesticated a female *Almas* named Zana. She was said to be violent toward her captor and was kept in a cage. Over the years, Zana was reportedly taught to perform tasks such as grinding grain and carrying firewood. However, witnesses said she never learned to speak the local language and became aggressive when dressed in clothing. Some skeptics believe Zana was likely a person from an isolated tribe of hunter-gatherers rather than one of the legendary wild creatures.

In 1963, Russian doctor Ivan Ivlov claimed to have spotted *Almas* again. While exploring the Altai Mountains in Russia, Ivlov saw three figures on a nearby slope. Through his binoculars, he observed that the figures moved like humans but were covered in hair. They appeared to be a family—two adults and a child—digging for food. Mongolian guides in Ivlov's group were familiar with these creatures and were not alarmed. When Ivlov spoke to local townspeople afterward, they seemed to accept the creatures as a normal part of the area's wildlife.

Cryptozoologist Dr. Marie-Jeanne Koffman spent her career studying the *Almas*. While she never proved their existence, Koffman collected dozens of footprints along with hair and stool samples. Her research estimates that the creatures weigh up to 500 lb. (230 kg) and could run at speeds up to 40 miles per hour (64 kph).

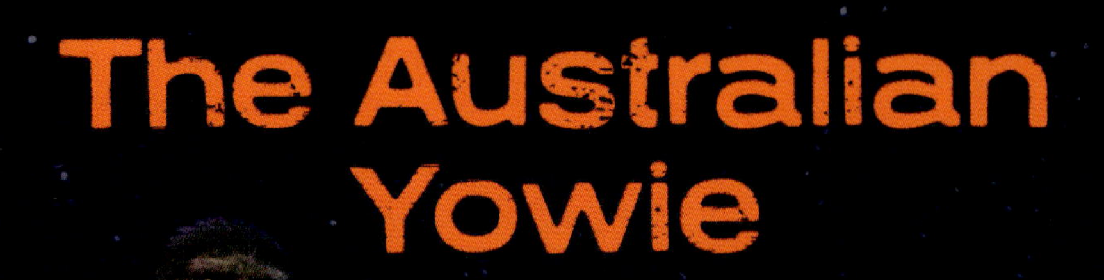

The Australian Yowie

The wooded hills and vast, dry deserts of eastern Australia are said to be home to a terrifying, humanlike being known as the Yowie. Hundreds of firsthand accounts from over the centuries describe a similar creature with dark fur, handlike paws, and a humanlike face with a wide mouth. Aboriginal Australians believed that the Yowie's large mouth was used to swallow people whole. The Yowie has a long and sometimes supernatural history among Australia's native peoples. Some, such as the Kuku Yalanji, claimed to live peacefully with the Yowie, while others, like the Ngunnawal, reported attacking and killing the creatures.

In 1882, naturalist H. J. McCooey reported seeing a Yowie at Batemans Bay in New South Wales. McCooey heard birds making loud noises and looked in their direction to see they were reacting to a Yowie sitting beneath them. He described the creature as having dirty, matted fur and long arms. McCooey said the Yowie was chattering back at the birds. The naturalist threw a rock at the Yowie, which then ran away.

Another Yowie sighting occurred in 1912. Charles Harper was camping with two friends on Currockbilly Mountain in New South Wales when he heard a low rumbling growl in the dark. After the group lit a campfire, they were able to see a huge, human-shaped animal pounding its furry chest and glaring at them with piercing dark eyes. Harper described the creature as standing just under 6 ft. (1.8 m) tall, with long, sharp canine teeth protruding from a large mouth. After watching the men for a few seconds, the creature ran away on all fours.

In 2021, Yowie researcher Dean Harrison claimed to have gotten proof of the creature's existence. Footage from Harrison's thermal cameras reportedly shows two creatures, each about 9 ft. (2.7 m) tall, hugging a tree to avoid being seen before fleeing the area. Harrison said the creatures made no noise as they fled. That same year, a truck driver reported seeing a Yowie on a small bridge in the Calgoa State Forest. The Yowie stared back at him before jumping over the side of the bridge and disappearing into the forest.

It is unclear how the Yowie received its name. Some think it stems from the Kámilarói word *Yō-wī*, which describes a spirit that roams the Earth at night. Others say it comes from the word *yahoo*, a name aboriginal Australians gave to an evil spirit.

One and the Same?

Stories of humanlike wild creatures, such as Bigfoot, the Yeti, and the Maricoxi, have existed in almost every culture around the world for centuries. Some people believe this widespread presence itself suggests these creatures must be real, but scientists argue that numerous eyewitness report alone are not enough to prove existence. Without physical evidence or clear uncontested photographic proof, it is difficult for scientists to confirm that these creatures are real.

Skeptics maintain that there is currently no strong evidence to support the existence of apelike cryptids. They believe that those who claim to have seen these creatures might be confusing them with other animals or might be involved in hoaxes designed to deceive and make a profit. They also point out that many of these reports come from times when technology and knowledge were limited. In today's era of smartphones, skeptics argue it is unlikely that such creatures have not been captured on clear footage by now

There are those, however, who still believe. They point out that scientists estimate there are 8.7 million unidentified species on Earth and claim these cryptids might simply be animals yet to be discovered. In Washington State alone, there are hundreds of mysterious casts of footprints found in nature that scientists have not been able to match to known animals. Some theories suggest that Bigfoot and other creatures could be descendants of prehistoric apes that migrated from Asia to North America during the Ice Age, making them distant relatives of creatures like the Yeti and the *Almas*. Many believe that encounters with these creatures may increase as human populations grow and continue to encroach on natural habitats. Whatever the truth, one thing is sure. The story of these apelike creatures is far from over!

According to the Bigfoot Field Researchers Organization, every state except Hawaii has had at least one reported sighting of Bigfoot. The organization has been notified of around 75,000 alleged sightings over the years, but it considers only about 6,000 of them to be from credible sources.

Glossary

Aboriginal the native peoples of Australia

Buddhist relating to an Asian religion or philosophy founded by Siddhartha Gautama in northeastern India in the 5th century BCE

canine teeth long, pointed teeth that are often the sharpest in the mouth

canyon a deep valley with steep sides, often carved by a river

cast a reproduction of something that has been created using a mold or form

controversy disagreement about something

credible able to be believed or trusted

cryptid an animal or creature that has been claimed to exist but of which there is no scientific proof

cryptozoologist a person who studies or searches for animals or beings whose existence has not been proven by science

culprit the person who is responsible for something happening

disputed something that people cannot reach an agreement on

DNA testing testing that is done to determine what a person or animal is made from

encounter a meeting, especially one that is unexpected

evidence objects or information that can be used to prove whether something is true

expedition a journey a group of people go on with a specific goal in mind

gait how someone walks

geologist a scientist who studies the structure and history of Earth

glimpse to get a brief look at something

gnawed worn down by being bitten or chewed on

hoax a trick or deception meant to fool people

investigators people who work to find out the facts or the truth about something

legacy a reputation that remains from an earlier time

legends stories that are passed down between people over a long period of time

matted tangled and packed tightly together

missionaries people sent on religious missions to other countries

monasteries religious buildings that are homes to priests, nuns, or monks

mysterious difficult to understand or explain; full of secrets

Neanderthal a humanlike species that lived from about 200,000 to 30,000 years ago

possesses takes control of someone or something

prehistoric relating to a time period before written records

profit money gained from something

prospectors people who search for valuable minerals, such as gold

pungent having a strong, often objectionable, odor

remote secluded or far removed from other things

retreated drew back to escape from danger

samples parts that are taken from something to be observed or tested

scalp the skin and hair on the top of a head

settlers people who move from one country to another

skeptics people who have an attitude of doubt or disbelief about something

special effects visual or sound effects introduced to a movie, video recording, or taped production

stool feces

supernatural something unusual, and often scary, that breaks the laws of nature

suspicions feelings or thoughts, often of uncertainty, about something

thermal cameras cameras that can detect the heat given off by nearby people or objects

tranquilizer guns weapons filled with darts that make people or animals who are shot fall asleep

witnessed saw something happen

zoologist a scientist who studies the behavior and biology of animals

Read More

Bahn, Christopher. *Bigfoot (Enduring Mysteries).* Mankato, MN: Creative Education, 2025.

Hubbard, Ben. *What Do We Know about the Yeti? (What Do We Know About?).* New York: Penguin Workshop, 2024.

Respicio, Mae. *Tracking Cryptids with Tech (Paranormal Tech).* North Mankato, MN: Capstone Press, 2024.

Teitelbaum, Michael. *Tracking Bigfoot: Is It Real or a Hoax? (X Books: Strange).* New York: Scholastic, Inc., 2020.

Learn More Online

1. Go to **FactSurfer.com** or scan the QR code below.
2. Enter "**Creatures Walking**" into the search box.
3. Click on the cover of this book to see a list of websites.

Index